VIBRATING AT THE SPEED OF LOVE
A Traveler's Meditation

By

Rosalie Cushman

Graphics by Richard Soledad

Also By Rosalie Cushman

The Man Confused by God

One Grasshopper's Journey

PREFACE

All my life I've had a strong sense of love. It has arrived in flashes, bathing me in an astoundingly pervasive sea, with me a mere drop. I have never been able to force the sense of it; it just comes of its own, spontaneously. In these later years, however, I have learned that certain conditions provide an easy environment in which it can erupt, triggered by anything from stunningly beautiful music, a sunset, the scent of flowers or trees, happy dogs, and being in the presence (in actuality or thought) of some people I hold dear.

Yet so much more of my waking life has not included love, other than the idea of it. I haven't always been operating from it, not in the actual state. Instead, my functionality has been driven by the ego with love relegated to a second-class citizenship, functioning more often than not as an abstraction, a concept, something to attain, but later. After all, there is a world of difference between "knowing about" something and "knowing," as wise men and avatars suggest. To know love is to be it, operating from the Source that claims us all.

Having known the state of love, however intermittent and brief, I find myself repeatedly drawn, sometimes intensely, while intermittently keeping it at bay in no less measure. You must wonder why after having experienced the blessed state one might postpone it. That presumed choice hasn't often been conscious. Instead, there has been a smokescreen of perceived loss, leaving me unaware yet driven by it nonetheless, vaguely feeling I could evaporate, albeit temporarily, if I were to surrender to Love completely.

This little book is an attempt to present both the learned 'facts' and the subjective experience between Love and the ego's struggle for dominance and definition. The format is designed to convey an East-West spiritual orientation, including both Judeo-Christian and Buddhist principles. While written in English, a hint of Chinese characters of love, peace, compassion, courage and others are reflected on opposing text pages as a feast for the eyes, subtly reminding the reader of Love's universality and oneness.

I have been heavily influenced by the teachings of Dr. David R. Hawkins as well as The Course in Miracles. Their works have dramatically expanded my understanding of Love along with its expression. In fact, both Dr. Hawkins and the Course have proved catalytic and profound for me, for which I remain indebted.

While not mentioned directly in this book, the additional trigger of love's expression throughout my lifetime has been my son, who has served as a monumental launch pad by his very essence, redirecting me back time and again to God's Love, which quite frankly permeates all things ceaselessly.

For Sam

魂

" I can see, and that is why I can be happy in what you call the dark, but which to me is golden. I can see a God-made world, not a man-made world."

– Helen Keller

This is the season for reconstituted living. Look at the smallest kindness and you will see the ingredients Einstein spoke of as comprising life. Love constitutes all things, abides in all things, reveals all things. It is never the catastrophe that does us in. Rather, it is the blind spot through which we view it.

Everything in the universe is connected to everything else. Essentially, there is only one Life here; one us. A sense of here-ness fades and is replaced by a state.

The state conveys a sense that Divinity is conspiring on one's behalf; a sense of being magnetically pulled to it. Surrender occurs without even understanding it is happening. At some point, however, awareness emerges. Complicity and a sense of choice, an agreement of sorts, become obvious, developing into a deeper surrendering when one is willing.

An infinite reality seems to scream "be quiet, make room, holiness is here."

What do you want to happen? The question presents itself inside. Operating from Spirit seems to be the obvious answer. It is beyond surrendering. It is an inner knowing, the ultimate comfort and security.

Yet fear may arise. Letting go of a presumed sense of self you thought was your source can be subtle and terrifying.

The struggle can be intense. It is not uncommon to stumble, alternating between two different states: fear versus courage, falseness versus truth, back and forth again until the more evolved state dominates.

愛

Pema Chodron says, "Usually we think that brave people have no fear. The truth is that they are intimate with fear." All too often intimacy is required, a kind of fear swamp to reach a state of intimacy before surrendering comes about. It's almost as if you have to be engulfed in it before it can dissipate.

楽

A greater awareness is required when acknowledging fear. It allows that there is a witness watching the thought of presumed danger. Spirit knows no such fear but the ego-mind thrives on it.

Fear and Love cannot coexist. One is false; the other true. They cannot both be true.

和

When you move away from fear to a new level of consciousness saturated with Love, you share it with the world – the universe. Everyone benefits; all are lifted.

Having caught the unmistakable fragrance, its magnanimity, power and purpose, Love's atom splits and generates an explosion that showers all things.

勇

The exact moment perception begins to change is subtle. It becomes clearer when a pattern emerges, accompanied by an awareness of thoughts as *antecedents*, with outcomes unfolding into form. Yet even a fraction of a second prior to the thought a feeling is observed, a lovingness.

At first the process seems like cause and effect. Then you learn this is not the case. Later, you come to know it is all one idea – *un*manifest made manifest. The seed does not cause the flower to be. The seed is the flower expressed differently in time. All is one event experienced as a differing perception.

魂

It slowly becomes apparent that there is a spirit in humankind that springs from one true Self. It is inherently available to us always, a substrate of existence. Compassion, gratitude, humility, stillness, and silence serve as mechanisms that facilitate awareness, interrupting habitual thoughts that generate fear.

Anytime there is gratitude something great is going on. By its very implication, all complaint, blame, projection slips away. What remains is Love with a capital L, an awareness of being part of something greater than one's self, a sense of *limitless* Spirit.

Anytime there is compassion for another's suffering Love expresses itself, generating relief even if no action is required. The field suffices.

Humility knows *of my own self, I can do nothing. All that I am comes from something greater than myself.*

Humility, gratitude and compassion come in the silence that is the effervescent field of awareness of Source, known to many as God.

章

When you give up trying to figure it all out, you are free to see what is really there, surrendering to something greater than what you *think* you see.

There is only one goal in this lifetime. It is to return to Spirit – not to die but to live from Truth. Everything is grist for the journey, the earthly context from which the soul rediscovers its Source.

愛

No matter what happens in life that might be defined as a tragedy, you go on being. It is not possible to really lose your life, the Self. The soul embodying the real Self is merely waiting to be recognized through Love, through awareness.

楽

The leaf holds together for Love, the bird sings its song for Love, the cloud forms for Love. The leaf, the bird, the cloud merely express their essence. They do not exist in terms of victim and perpetrator, villain or savior. They just *are*. And so too are we. That's all there is; discrete beings swimming in an infinite field of Love.

There is a natural contentment in Being. It comes from the vein of existence that is rooted in the heart. The most delicious aspect of it seems to be that it just "is" for no particular reason other than its *own* expression as the thing itself. It is gripping.

和

There are times in life, when meeting someone or talking with someone, that Divinity is apparent, obvious. It is miraculous when this is recognized as connectedness, Oneness.

奥

It is exquisite when one is unable to discern whether one is sending Love or receiving Love. A feeling of both transpires. Allness is experienced; a singular transaction.

魂

Later, it is remarkably liberating when one realizes all that is needed is to be loving. The awareness of involuntary loving generates and expands being loved.

At times Love seems forgotten. Where does it go? The ego has suppressed its impulse. Love waits, ever patient for recognition and reclamation.

Then the intuition arrives. Do nothing, there is nothing *to* do.

The shame of ego reliance surfaces; just as quickly, it is gone. *Gone!*
It has been taken, replaced by forgiveness and exquisite Love.

There is nothing Holiness cannot do. It reverses the laws of the physical world when one is willing to suspend all judgment. First, however, surrender is required.

慈

Holiness inhabits us. At times there is awareness of this fact. All other presumed identities are a fabrication, yet still we cling. The only thing to be done is to *let go* of the clinging.

章

There is nothing more rapturous than hearing *I love you* echoing in the interior, unable to differentiate between subject and object. All that is clear is a tremendous comfort in this state; a knowingness. It is an immersion, presenting itself as both an origin and a return.

Love is peaceful, although peace requires adjustment, for it has not been operational, let alone consciously recognized or sought. Yet it arrives as a quality of Love, unbidden, of its own accord.

愛

Love's unfolding is going on all the time. One must look constantly, really look, to see as Helen Keller.

楽

Love becomes evident. It requires assent. All you have to do is *decide* and *the door will open.*

Again, there comes a palpable uplift with words forming inside, saying, *I love you.* For the first time, in a flash, it becomes truly known.

和

It is utterly remarkable, when gazing into someone's eyes and feeling overwhelming Love for another and know it in truth for the first time. It comes from a Source greater than you but of which you are a part. There is a suspension of separation. In fact, *IT passes through your being.* It *is* your being, it is the Presence. It is not subject to reason or logic. Love exists in a field of expression that is not of mind.

Often, the state of happiness and joy generates fear. We say we love joy, even crave it and then upon its arrival, we cut it off. Joy is our natural state. Not so for the ego. The ego's natural state is fear and conquering. Assenting to Love and the joy and peace it generates is a Grace.

魂

It is a challenge to let go of fear when you think it has served you in some way. Yet in the end it is harder to hang onto it.

We all inform one another about our connection. It's the light in the eye, the touch that lingers, the compassion transmitted during a crisis. Michelangelo had it right. What appears to be only space between the fingertips of God to Adam is in Truth filled with the energy of Love. Quite simply, it is the original *transmission*. It is the *only* transmission.

Happiness and joy occur when you look at the actions of the ego and laugh, knowing it is not you; such sweet relief!

The shelf life of Love is one divided by zero – Infinity.

慈

At a certain stage, you recognize it takes far too much energy to operate from ego. Even though the ego will put up quite a fight, Love will draw you in. A slow and steady functioning from a greater Self will become recognizable, building on its own momentum.

You make great progress when you give up thinking as a primary activity and instead rely on lovingness. When thinking ceases dominion, Love rushes in.

It is not because you are so holy that you are loved. Rather, it is because you are Holiness itself.

愛

The journey need not be so complicated, but we love the thrill, the intoxication of presumed authorship of our lives. It is only when we become aware of the Presence that we experience an exhilaration of such magnitude, such gravity that we cannot help but surrender.

楽

There are moments when Love feels so overwhelming, so staggering that the impulse is to shut it down. Fear of youness being lost erupts until it is remembered that Love is the very thing that you seek and it's all you are in Truth.

U pon waking one morning, there was a door. It opened to reveal an abundance of light, white and all-encompassing. The light was comforting, radiant, welcoming. It stretched from here to infinity; its invitation could not be denied. "Come," It said. "This is your natural state – the sea in which you wake."

和

You need not ever receive less than was given to you in Truth. It is only perception that distorts your thinking, that you are anything less than infinite Love. You cannot return the gift, only delay its receipt.

The ego would delay recognition of Divinity as long as possible. When catching glimmers of the ego's charade it becomes apparent that there is only one thing going on here, one unified field of Love. It is magnificence; it is Grace.

魂

It is critical to see things in a different light. Fear of punishment for relying on the ego's falsity can seem like a force to be reckoned with since the ego is heavily invested in judgment. Once challenged, however, its days are numbered. Not to worry, the energy of Love carries only forgiveness – the bridge to the other side.

There it is again! The knowingness of Love seeks us out and finds us, like a homing device.

Think back to when you were three or five years old. There is a quality, an essence of self that has remained constant. That original essence is the traveler seeking home. As the field of Love makes claim, the distance shortens and a doorway to it appears.

The Traveler is the One seeing the doorway.

慈

All becomes bright as the Traveler enters Light.

華

The Traveler is absorbed in Light.

The Traveler *is* the Light.

愛

The Traveler is the One.

ABOUT THE AUTHOR

Rosalie attended Boston University before graduating from Iowa State University in 1985, where she earned her bachelor's degree in English with a minor in Political Science. She has been a freelance writer since 2008, authoring two memoirs, writing articles for San Diego's lifestyle periodical, Fine Magazine, as well as drafting Search Engine Optimization content for Wpromote, Inc, and the Carlsbad Manufacturing Group. Rosalie has also taught memoir and expository writing in the past. Prior to writing and teaching, she enjoyed twenty years in public relations and marketing for all things books, first for a library and then Borders Books & Music. She enjoys small town living, the thud of fruit as it hits the ground, cows and chickens and, oh yes, the crisp clean air of Northern California where she resides.

Richard Soledad has worked in the creative field for over a decade. To this day, he swears that he has been able to draw a perfect circle at least once in his life, and considers this his crowning achievement. Despite popular belief, he is actually a nice guy. Sometimes. Among other things, he loves to draw and paint as well as explore Northern San Diego County with his wife and daughters.

Made in the USA
Lexington, KY
22 November 2019